AWESOME ADVENTURE

By **Melaina Faranda**
Illustrated by **Paul Könye**

Pearson Australia
(a division of Pearson Australia Group Pty Ltd)
707 Collins Street, Melbourne, Victoria 3008
PO Box 23360, Melbourne, Victoria 8012
www.pearson.com.au

First published 2010 by Pearson Australia

2019 2018 2017 2016
10 9 8 7 6 5 4 3 2

Publisher: Simone Calderwood
Editor: Anne McKenna
Designer: Kim Ferguson
Project Editor: Aisling Coughlan
Copyright & Pictures Editor: Caitlin O'Brien
Production Controller: Claire Henry
Illustrator: Paul Könye

Printed in Australia by the SOS Print + Media Group

ISBN 978 1 4425 2440 8

Pearson Australia Group Pty Ltd ABN 40 004 245 943

Contents

Chapter 1

"I Never Wanted to Come Here!"

David wished that they had never come here. He pressed his face to the rain-streaked window as the car slipped down the dirt driveway to take them to school. Lantana vines scratched the doors and grass seeds showered the bonnet. Another day in paradise—yeah, right.

If only they could go back home. Back to their real home—a house that had doors and windows and rooms. Not a cramped tin shed with a roller door, mouldy squares of carpet and no privacy! And forget TV or playing computer games. Here there was only solar power.

Mum had sold his video game console at a garage sale a week before they left for thirty measly dollars. He hadn't even been given the money—it got used on petrol for the long drive up here, to their new place.

"Whatcha thinking, Baby Davy?" Mum asked, as the four-wheel-drive slid back and forth in a slick of orange mud.

Lena sniggered from the front passenger seat.

David scowled. "Do you think it will clear up in time for us to go to the Awesome Adventure Centre this weekend?" Dad had promised to take him. It was two hours away and supposed to be really cool—with an outdoor climbing wall and 3D laser games.

Know-it-all Lena shook her head. "It's going to flood for sure. The tree frogs are making that 'ark ark ark' sound. Plus, the black cockatoos have been screeching. It means there's going to be more rain."

"What are you—Jungle Girl or something?"

"I just pay attention. I'm not brain dead like you."

"Lena," Mum warned. "Love is all there is, remember?"

"Oh, *puh-leeze*!" Lena said. She rested back into the seat and put the earplugs from her MP3 player back in.

"She's right, though," Mum said, gripping the steering wheel with white knuckles, as they crossed the causeway. Already, a thick skin of creek water flowed over it. They hit another bump and Yappa slid off David's lap. The fox terrier scrambled back up, leaving a trail of muddy paw prints on his jeans.

Yappa glanced at David with reproachful eyes.

"It's not my fault," David mouthed back at Yappa. "I never wanted to come here either."

"The ants are going crazy, too," Mum continued. "They're all through the cupboards. You kids will be eating peanut butter and ant sandwiches for your school lunch today. Bit more protein."

Yuck! This was what it had been like ever since they had moved here. There were creatures everywhere—bush rats in the rafters, mud wasps in the cupboards, mosquitoes whining around their mozzie nets, frogs in the shower, even a red-bellied black snake in the toilet!

If only they hadn't left the city. David had been happy riding his skateboard down at the park with Yappa trotting behind. And on rainy days he could hole up in his room, "the bat cave" Dad called it, and play computer games or check out the latest extreme skating moves on the Internet.

He should have paid more attention to all the farming magazines littering Mum's desk. Perhaps then he could have tried to stop his parents. Tell them it was insane moving away from the city. What if one of them got sick and they couldn't get to a hospital? Or he could have started a guilt campaign to make them feel terrible about pulling him out of school, where he had heaps of friends.

But it had come as a complete shock when Mum and Dad had told him that they were moving to the middle of nowhere for a tree change! They were going to live in paradise, with fruit trees, pure water and soil so good they would be eating cabbage-sized tomatoes.

Lena hadn't minded. She didn't have many friends and was happy to curl up and read a book anywhere. And she actually liked going for walks and learning about frogs, snakes and all the other animals they shared their shed with!

But there was nothing exciting to do in the country. There were no smooth road surfaces for his skateboard, so it was already covered in cobwebs and mouse poo in a corner of the shed. He had resented their move from the very start—and there was one thing he really didn't like... his school.

Chapter 2

Ms Bonaventure or the Bus?

"**Here we are,**" Mum said, pulling up outside the entrance to the old wooden school buildings.

Ms Bonaventure stood at the gate, ushering in soggy kids beneath a bright orange umbrella that had googly eyes and a tail like a goldfish.

When she saw David, she beamed at him beneath unnaturally red hair, as if he was her favourite pupil. Which probably wasn't that unlikely, given that the school only had fifty kids!

David rolled his eyes. His old school had been a three-storey brick building with lots of classrooms and hundreds of kids, and there had been computers in every room. Some of the kids had even brought their laptops to school. In the playground, there had been real basketball courts and a proper oval.

Lena smirked as David scrambled out of the car and into a deep puddle that soaked his shoes. She was catching the bus to the secondary school from further up the road.

"See you this afternoon," Mum said, blowing him a kiss.

"Yeah, try to spot me in the crowd," David muttered.

"Yap," Yappa agreed.

Mum ignored them. "Have to dash and hang out the washing."

"Very funny," groaned David.

He looked up at the sky—it was the same as it had been for the past three weeks—filled with heavy grey clouds that reminded him of the scratchy blankets they'd had on school camps.

If only the rain would clear so that Dad could still take him to the Awesome Adventure Centre. There was nothing to do in the country; it was boring.

"I hope you remembered to bring your lunch today, David?" Ms Bonaventure sang out.

David cringed. Lunch. That would be the ant and peanut butter sandwich. What had his parents been thinking when they decided to move here?

The bell rang, sharp and shrill through the thundering rain. They had already finished recess and were in the middle of a maths test.

The class cheered and the kids erupted from their seats. They stuffed their pencil cases and workbooks into their bags, and put their chairs on their tables.

"What's going on?" David asked Jarrah.

Jarrah was the boy Ms Bonaventure had made him sit next to. His dad was one of the traditional Indigenous owners of the country. Like David, they lived up Joey Road.

"Saved by the bell!" Jarrah whooped.

His dark eyes shone with excitement. "It's because of the rain. It means the emergency buses have come to take us home before we get cut off by the creeks. You coming or what?"

David shrugged. "Mum usually picks me up, but she'll still be at home. I don't know how I'm going to let her know, because our phone line went down a few days ago. A branch fell on it and the guys who are meant to fix it haven't been out yet." *And*, he thought, *she got rid of her mobile phone when we moved to this so-called paradise.*

Jarrah joined the rest of the class, who were barging out of the door. Even Ms Bonaventure had packed up her basket with books, her tea mug and the bunch of bright orange flowers from the vase on her desk. She bustled about securing windows and straightening desks.

"You should come on the bus," Jarrah called back to David. "Otherwise you could get stranded."

Confused, David followed Jarrah outside to the school gates. Who could he stay with if he got stranded? He didn't know anyone around here, not properly, and even though some of the kids had been friendly, he'd kept his distance.

If he could make his parents believe he couldn't make friends at the new school, then maybe, just maybe, they'd agree to go back home. After all, their house in the city hadn't sold yet. He could have his own room again. And after being up here, he would really know how to appreciate a new DVD player, computer and TV…

Jarrah looked around and a wicked gleam shone from his eyes. "If you get stuck here, you'll probably have to stay with Ms Bonaventure."

Ms Bonaventure was conducting the chaos of kids with her googly-eyed fish umbrella and singing instructions in a warbling soprano, like an opera singer.

"I'll get the bus," said David.

Chapter 3

What Would Bart Do?

Kids were laughing, shouting and jumping up and down in the aisles. Mr Singh, the bus driver, stopped the bus and told everyone to sit down. But as soon as he started driving again, it was chaos. David couldn't believe that the bus had a DVD player, but everyone except him was ignoring *The Simpsons* playing on the TV at the front.

He was spellbound. The horrible soupy grey sky faded away as he got lost in a world of bright yellow people. What would Bart have done if Homer and Marge had moved him to the middle of nowhere?

Usually the drive to school seemed so long, but it felt like only a couple of minutes had passed when Jarrah shook his shoulder.

"You gonna get off here?"

David reluctantly broke his gaze from the screen. He hefted his school bag and followed Jarrah and his two younger sisters, Missy and Rose, off the bus at the turn-off into Joey Road.

Rain pelted down, drilling holes into the torrent of brown water that flowed over the causeway. Only a few hours before, it had been a steady trickle. Now it was a raging white-flecked river.

Jarrah waded in carefully. “The current’s too strong,” he announced. “I could get across, but Missy and Rose are too little. We could cut some bark and make a canoe.”

Missy rolled her eyes. “Yeah, right, you’ve been watching too many movies. We could shout for Dad to bring the tractor down.”

Jarrah ignored her. “Best thing is for me to go overland up around the back of Fogarty’s place and get Dad to come back down with the tractor. You wait here.”

It wasn’t a suggestion. It was a command. Jarrah’s dark hair and saturated green shirt gradually faded into the bush until he disappeared.

David scuffed a sneaker awkwardly in the wet red clay. Missy and Rose were younger than him and they were girls. He had no idea what to say to them.

Instead, David started shouting, just in case Mum or Dad could hear him—"Mum! Dad!"—but the rushing water drowned out his calls.

Over the river's roar came a sharp bark. A fox terrier hurtled down the muddy road and appeared on the other side of the swollen creek. Yappa! David wondered if he could get the dog to take a message to his parents further up the hill. Maybe three lots of yips and yaps, like an SOS in Morse code!

David called again and, at the sound of his master's voice, the terrier hurled himself into the creek. The little dog paddled hard, but the current was swift and strong. He desperately poked his snout into the air, but a wash of tangled sticks covered him.

Yappa vanished.

"NOOOOO!" shouted David. He watched in horror as a glimpse of white beneath the muddy surface streaked down the swollen creek bed.

Chapter 4

Yappa

"**Don't go in!**" Missy yelled.

David raced along the bank, ignoring the lantana vines scratching his bare face and arms. He narrowly missed tripping over tree roots as he tore along.

He spotted a mini whirlpool further downstream where leaves and sticks collected in a swirl of foam against a large, slimy boulder. The causeway was back around a couple of bends and he could no longer see Missy or Rose.

Clinging to the slippery rock, David lowered himself into the water. It was warm and smelled of earth. He wedged a foot between two rocks so that he wouldn't be swept away.

The creek carried Yappa towards him. The little dog's snout pushed through the water into the air.

David reached out his hand as far as it would go. Yappa was almost within reach ...

Straining his fingers until they hurt, David just managed to hook a finger in Yappa's collar and pull the terrier close. The little dog lay limp in his arms, its eyes closed. It was pitiful how skinny Yappa looked with soaked fur.

A hot sting of salt pricked David's eyes. The last time he had cried was when everything had been packed into cardboard boxes, and the removalists came.

He had lost his home and now he had lost his only true friend. And it was his fault. If only he hadn't called out.

He remembered Yappa as a pup. They had got him from the RSPCA. Yappa had been shaking and coughing and he was so tiny he could have stood on the palm of Dad's hand, except that Dad hadn't wanted him. As far as he was concerned, dogs didn't fit into Australia's natural ecosystems.

But who would have guessed that one tiny little dog could have so much spark?

It was Yappa who had been the best cricket fielder ever.

Yappa who had sat under the computer desk, nipping toes to get the family to take him for a walk.

Yappa who had alerted them to the huntsman spider in the garage.

David had even caught Dad giving Yappa the odd pat when he thought no-one else could see.

As the water swirled around him, David cradled the cold little body high against his chest and finally allowed himself to sob.

He cried for Yappa, and for himself because he finally understood that he would never be going home.

Then something warm and rough slid against his chin.

David opened his eyes.

The tongue darted back again. Yappa gazed up with concerned black eyes.

"Yappa! You're okay!"

David carefully placed the little dog on top of the boulder before trying to pull himself up. His fingers slipped off the slimy moss and his foot wedged further in between the rocks. He gave a fierce, sharp pull. His foot twisted painfully and lodged further.

He was stuck.

Chapter 5

Stuck!

David took a deep breath and tried to use both hands to free his foot. The rocks had been jammed into place by something slimy and hard—a log.

On the boulder above, Yappa picked himself up, shook a spray of droplets into the air and barked. A sodden stalk of grass hung from his jaw. He cocked his head to one side, puzzled.

"I can't move," David whispered. "I'm stuck."

Yappa sent up a volley of barks, dancing back and forth on his small paws.

"I can't do it," David said. His heart thudded and his mouth went dry. He cried out for help but his words were drowned by the water's roar. Drifts of matted sticks and debris edged up around his ribcage, which a minute before had been above water. David scooped away the sticks in panic. He was not imagining it—the creek was rising.

He tried to keep his body upright as a steady scum of leaves and twigs swirled and banked against him. What if Missy and Rose had thought he'd kept running alongside the river to join Jarrah? What if Jarrah's dad had already come and gone on the tractor?

The water felt colder as it crept closer to his shoulders. A chill shuddered through him. How long did he have before the creek rushed over his head? He yanked at his leg again, moaning with pain as his foot twisted further. His toe shifted slightly. David tried one almighty wrench.

The boulder rolled closer, seeming to crush his foot. He yelled, his face screwing up with agony—he had never felt this much pain.

Yappa jumped back and forth, growling and barking at the water, as if he was warning it to stay away.

"Yappa, you've got to get help."

The terrier dug his claws deeper into the moss and wouldn't meet David's gaze.

David desperately looked around. He didn't want to drown. He tried to calculate the width of the creek. He was stuck in a bend and it made the watercourse narrower, not like the broad, ruffled sheets of water that knocked the reeds flat on all the straight stretches. Was it possible?

David twisted his upper body to reach the terrier. He seized Yappa and held him close. The little dog wagged his stubby tail and licked David's face ecstatically.

With a sob, David took careful aim, and threw his dog across the creek.

Yappa landed in shallow water. He leapt onto the bank and shook himself before turning to David with sad eyes.

"Go, Yappa! Go home!" David ordered. He tried to make his voice mean. "Go on home."

Yappa gazed at him with a puzzled look.

"Get out of here!"

The terrier scrambled up the vine-tangled bank and left David behind.

Chapter 6

Help Me!

"**Breathe,**" **David** said to himself. The water lapped beneath his chin. He could taste dirt at the back of his throat. The canopy of trees and vines almost closed above him, leaving only a thin, snaking gap of grey sky.

Across the creek, a brown bird was taking shelter beneath a broad green leaf the colour of the Granny Smith apple in his lunchbox. The bird tucked its smooth, graceful head into a puffed chest of feathers. It was a beautiful colour, like the cocoa-dusted chocolate Mum got from the health food store. He wished he knew what the bird was called. Lena would know.

David pictured the stricken looks on his parents' faces when the creek went back down and they found his body with his foot still trapped between the rocks. Mum would stagger back and her skin would go white, like the time she got the phone call about Gran's stroke.

He couldn't bear it. He wanted to live. But Yappa hadn't come back. And neither had anyone else. Even if Yappa had gone home soaking wet, Mum and Dad wouldn't think anything of it. They had no idea that David had caught an early bus home. They were probably sitting around planning the orchard, occasionally getting up to stoke the combustion stove to bake Anzac biscuits for when David and Lena got home.

The muddy water lapped his bottom lip, seeking entrance through the down-turned corners of his lips. A tiny leaf crept in and he spat it out before tilting his head back to stare into the sky. His ears filled with water and rain fell into his eyes. He blinked rapidly and couldn't bring himself to close them.

To be cold, trapped *and* in the dark was too terrifying.

A distant sound reached his ears through the water. Not the gurgle and tinkle of stones shifting or sticks and logs scraping the creek bed, but something rhythmic and steadily growing louder. He tried turning his head to the side and promptly swallowed a mouthful of brown water.

Tears welled in his eyes, blurring the dark trees above just as the first film of water washed over his mouth. He raised his head and called out hoarsely, "Help! Help me!" His voice sounded muted to his waterlogged ears.

"*Daaaaaviiiid! Daaaaaaviiiid!*" The voices were faint.

"Here! I'm over here!" he screamed, but a rush of water invaded his throat and his nostrils.

David heard a sharp bark. Then non-stop barking. Closer and closer. No. The noise. It didn't belong. He closed his eyes. Cold darkness rushed over him.

Chapter 7

The Rescue

Something tugged him from a dream —golden sunlight streaming through the trees from a blue sky.

A sharp pain darted through his body. Then he felt big, strong arms pulling him up, and the throbbing heaviness around his foot suddenly shifted away.

He landed like a fish, belly first, onto the slimy boulder and was turned sideways. A finger felt inside his mouth, pressing against his tongue.

A hot rush of weed-stinking water vomited out of him. He could hear voices all around.

David's eyes fluttered open. He dimly made out a dark, wiry figure with gentle brown eyes.

He lifted his head. There was another man, climbing out of the water—Dad!

Two girls were on the embankment and slightly apart from them, closer to the creek, stood Jarrah, his eyes wide and scared.

"I told you," Missy said. "The dog was telling us where he was."

"Bless that little mutt," Dad whispered, pulling David against his soaked T-shirt and cradling him close. "Promise me," he whispered into David's hair, "promise me you'll never go anywhere near a flooded creek again."

David nodded, grabbed hold of Yappa and squeezed his thanks.

The tractor chugged back through the bush. David rested back against Dad, while Jarrah, Rose and Missy leaned out over the side, ducking their heads whenever they were about to be hit by a branch.

When the roller door shed came into view, Jarrah's father pulled the tractor to a stop, but left it idling.

Dad helped David climb off the tractor.

"You're all going to come in for a cuppa, aren't you?" Dad insisted.

The other man grinned and turned off the engine.

Mum came to the door. "What are you doing back from school, David? You're soaking! What on earth hap—?"

"Long story." Dad carried David inside. "Let's get these wet things off and warm you up."

Chapter 8

Awesome!

David listened to everyone introducing themselves. By the time he had changed into dry clothes and emerged from behind the sheet that partitioned off his bed from the rest of the shed, everyone was sitting at the big round table. They were cradling hot drinks and eating freshly baked Anzac biscuits.

David sat in front of the combustion stove and warmed his chilled fingers. They were wrinkled and white.

Something was different. He looked up and realised that Dad had fixed the roof so the constant drip of water into a bucket had stopped.

"So now, will someone please tell me exactly what happened?" Mum demanded.

David glanced at Dad. "You might not want to hear this."

Mum's eyes narrowed. "Hear what?"

"Yappa fell in the creek and I tried to save him. But I got stuck."

"You did *what*!"

Dad cut in. "The little mutt found me in the wood shed and latched on to my trousers. I thought he was going to rip the hem off. I told him to scat, but he kept tugging at my hem like he wanted me to go with him. So I followed him down to the creek and ran into John and Jarrah on the tractor. John said he was picking up the kids."

"And when they came, we told them how David had gone after the dog!" Missy exclaimed, not wanting to miss out. "I guessed that the dog was trying to tell us where David was."

Mum slowly put down her mug of tea and went around to where David sat shivering in front of the fire.

"Yappa would have drowned, Mum," he said, desperately. "I couldn't let that happen." David squeezed his eyes shut to stop the tears coming in front of Missy, Rose and Jarrah.

"I never wanted to come here and Yappa's my only friend."

David glanced at Jarrah, who looked away.

"I want you to understand three things, David," Mum said, gently. "The first is that we are never going back to live in the city again. We've had an offer on the house and have accepted it. The house has been sold.

"The second thing is that we will be building another house right here when the money comes through."

She put her hand on his cheek and smiled. "One that's big enough for you to have a room of your own, Baby Davy, and enough solar power to run a decent laptop."

"If we ever see the sun again," Dad added.

"What's the third thing?" David asked.

"You must never, never, *never* go into a flooded creek again," Mum said. "Or I'll throw the laptop into it after you."

"Can he go in a bark canoe, though?" Jarrah asked.

"Or a tyre tube?" Missy added.

"No-one will be crossing the creek for the next couple of days," Jarrah's dad said, firmly.

"Maybe David can come over this weekend instead?" asked Jarrah.

"Yeah, can I go, please?" David begged.

"But what about the Awesome Adventure Centre?" Dad reminded him.

"Um, I don't really feel like any more adventures right now."

"As long as you're still up for making a canoe and hunting goannas," Jarrah said, with a cheeky grin.

Missy rolled her eyes, "Or you could just have a go on the trail bikes."

David laughed. "Deal!"